A TESTIMONIAL TO GRACE

A Testimonial
to Grace

by

Avery Dulles

SHEED and WARD
New York, 1946

NIHIL OBSTAT
>Edward G. Murray, D.D.
Censor Librorum

IMPRIMATUR
✠ Richard J. Cushing, D.D.
Archbishop, Boston

Boston, Ascension Thursday, 1946.

For

WILLIAM F. MACOMBER

Fellow-wayfarer

FOREWORD

I have often been asked why I became a Catholic. The only sufficient cause for any conversion is, of course, divine grace, for which man can give no explanation. But since grace normally operates by supplying impetus to the will and light to the mind, the question can be answered, on the natural plane, by rendering an account of one's personal motivations. This I was never able to do at all adequately until, thanks to a period of relative leisure at sea during World War II, I had an opportunity to reflect somewhat carefully on the processes by which my ideas had evolved. At that time I set down the reminiscences here published.

The narrative falls, chronologically, into two sections, devoted respectively to the search for sound philosophic values and to the scrutiny of religious doctrines. The formation of my views on these matters will, I trust, be of interest to others who are not unwilling to face those fundamental philosophic and religious problems which have ever been the chief concern of the wise. For it is a task of theirs, as it has been of mine, to establish their own position in relation to those systems of thought—such as skepticism, materialism, and liberalism—which, as I have tried to indicate, hold almost unchallenged sway in our secular universities and thus set the tenor of our intellectual life.

Cambridge, Mass.
20 May 1946.   **A.D.**

PART I

A TESTIMONIAL TO GRACE

I entered Harvard College in the fall of 1936, having been trained in one of the "better" non-sectarian boarding schools of New England. At that time I possessed, like most of my comrades, a fairly complete but equally naive philosophy of life, founded on a variety of popular superstitions of a type all too often infused into adolescent minds by well-meaning teachers of physics, history, and literature.

In the first place, I considered it a proved fact that the original and uncreated reality, the sufficient cause of the whole universe, was physical matter, presumably in the form of irreducible atoms or ever circling electronic particles. Following the laws of its own nature, this primeval matter had apparently, at some unspecified period in the remote past, congregated into certain large globular masses. From one such mass, that whirling ball of fire called the sun, our earth had chanced to be cast off, and on our cooling planet, by a further accident, life had emerged. Eventually, through an indefinitely repeated process of variation and natural selection, life had, it seemed, evolved into its human form.

It did not enter my mind to consider that the world owed its existence to a wise Creator, that a beneficent Providence watched over and directed it, or that the soul, as the loving work of God's hands, possessed an eternal destiny. When I contemplated death, as I not infrequently did, I was never troubled by Hamlet's fear of finding there anything different from the peace of oblivion. I took it for granted that the human spirit was completely dependent for its existence and operation on the life of the body. The workings of the spirit, including the processes of thought itself, I considered to be a pale reflection of interrelated physical activities in the brain.

The religious and moral aspects of such a cosmology are only too obvious. Manifestly, there was in it no room for God. Every notion of God was in my opinion a sort of *deus ex machina,* an invention of the human mind to explain away facts which could not be otherwise accounted for. Just as scientific progress had, as I imagined, made it unnecessary to assume that God periodically intervened in the universe, so too, I inferred, it was gradually becoming superfluous to posit a supernatural First Winder of the universal clock.

Man having been produced by chance, it seemed illusory to hold that he had any ordained end or was subject to any moral strictures not of his own making. Morality, then, could be interpreted as a texture of conventions woven by the ingenuity of men for reasons of convenience. "Revealed" religion I dismissed as a vain attempt to find sanctions (where none in truth existed) for such conduct and mental attitudes as proved conducive to social well-being.

I regarded it as a rather unfortunate fact that, in view of the progress of science—and especially, for some obscure reason, the discovery of evolution—intelligent men could no longer believe in the immortality of the human soul. As a result, I judged, supernatural religion was now relegated to the realm of superstition, and morality exposed in its true guise, as a sort of social contract expressive of the general desires of the community. No longer did there exist any power which could be invoked to deter the contracting parties from cheating a little to their own advantage—other than the risk of being caught and penalized by their fellow men. And in view of the lawlessness of the universe,

I could feel little indignation against those who violated a few clauses of the ethical code.

Though not personally a great cheater at the game of life, I adhered to my own premises logically enough to be frankly out for myself alone. I considered it a platitude that everyone, by an irresistible law of his being, sought only his own personal satisfaction, and that "unselfishness" must consequently be regarded as either hypocrisy or insanity. A moderate respect for the aspirations of others was, however, a necessary concomitant of enlightened self-interest.

The "happiness" which was the universal object of human endeavor might, in my judgment, be sought under any of a number of forms. Some, to be sure, bent their efforts to obtaining merely the grosser forms of pleasure, but for my part, while I did not condemn these others, I never identified happiness exclusively with ease or sensual delight. The romantic element was strong enough in my nature to persuade me that there existed a deeper kind of happiness, from which struggle was never absent. The eternal servitude of Prometheus, whom naught could compel to yield to the gods, seemed to me to represent a more valid conception of heaven than did the eternal bliss of the angels. To par-

take fully of life was, I believed, to strive un-
ceasingly like Goethe's Faust. To be content,
on the other hand, was in a sense to die.

The Promethean heritage, the fire of the
gods, seemed to be immortalized in the arts;
and I was greatly devoted to painting and
poetry, though I had no ear for music. Art I
revered as the expression of the divine element,
the everlasting prize of joy in conflict, by the
acquisition of which man rises above himself.
In art I found preserved and canonized the
deepest and most sublime experience of man,
and depth of personal experience was for me
identical with human excellence. Success in
life, I held with Walter Pater, was to burn always with a "hard, gemlike flame."

This rapturous delight, this elixir of life, had
nothing in common with savage fury or animal
contentment. The passions of the many were
lacking in glamor, elegance, and subtlety. For
the desires and tenets of the vast majority I
felt an indifference coupled with a touch of
Ibsen's contempt.[1] The rarified excellence which
I esteemed was passion distilled by the white
heat of its own intensity and crystallized in last-

---

[1] As expressed, for example, in *An Enemy of the
People.*

ing form by creative achievement on the intellectual plane. This chemical refinement of emotion was, I noted, most perfectly effected in the isolation of the proverbial ivory tower. The tranquil ecstasy of the "escapists" aroused my admiration and enthusiasm. My favorite painter was the retiring Cézanne. Arthur Rimbaud and Wallace Stevens had achieved in verse the esoteric quality which I admired.

My political ideas, if I can be said to have had ideas on a subject which I regarded as insufferably prosaic, were summed up in a solemn dislike for regimentation. The rapid advance of collectivized production was hateful to me because it threatened to engender a society which supplied neither stimulus nor outlet for artistic energies. The anesthetizing routine of the average life, which dulled the artistic sensibilities and inhibited the creative ferment in the individual spirit, was the epitome of all that I rebelled against. The notion of discipline from any quarter—and above all from the ineluctable power of the State—aroused my resentment. My Utopia was a society which gave to each the freedom to seek his own brand of happiness, and to the élite the opportunity of stealing fire from the gods. The best government, I would recite, is that which governs least. Mill's *Essay on Liberty* was my political *Credo*.

My first year in college did little to upset the scheme of values which I had formulated and espoused while in preparatory school. During this year I studied no philosophy course, and from the courses in history and literature which I attended I imbibed only the positivism of Auguste Comte, which served to entrench me further in materialism. I felt a vague sympathy for every social movement styled as "liberal," and read with uncritical veneration the political manifestos of such diverse authors as Thomas Mann, André Malraux, and Ernest Hemingway.

Desisting somewhat from artistic pursuits, I took up at this time the cult of what is called "experience." As a result, my freshman year was a wild and chaotic year, marked by an excess of drinking and a corresponding deficiency of sleep. My room, distinguished by the possession of a percolator, became a center of nocturnal revelry. Whole nights were passed in aimless jocularity either here or in shoddy Boston bars. My attendance at classes was casual at best.

This manner of life was abruptly altered in April, at which time two of my closest friends were expelled from college as the result of a midnight adventure in which the Boston police saw fit to intervene. I myself narrowly escaped expulsion for complicity in the same offense: the University's Administrative Board having reached a favorable decision in my case thanks to the swinging of a single vote in the third ballot of their deliberations. After that incident I settled down a little, chastened perhaps by the narrowness of this escape, but also convinced by trial and error that I could derive little satisfaction from engaging in disorderly escapades.

My nearest friend, after my two less fortunate comrades had been dismissed, was not a university student but a waiter on the night shift in a Cambridge cafeteria which was one of my customary nocturnal haunts. Frank Stacy was a Cambridge lad about my own age. His background was one of poverty and squalor, but, endowed with a fine and ever active mind, he had read widely, and combined in his person the gifts of a keen intelligence and a thoroughly engaging manner. He and I would meet regularly about three o'clock in the morning, at which time he got off from work, and pass the hours from then until the beginning of my morning classes discussing eagerly the works of Dylan Thomas, James Joyce, and other contemporary writers of poetry and fiction. Born and bred a Catholic, Stacy had lost his faith, and I certainly did little to restore it to him. I remember being genuinely amazed when in an unguarded moment he ventured the opinion that man, being possessed of reason, was specifically different from the other animals—a little suggestion which the good sisters had left with him in his childhood. Every educated person, I had imagined, understood that there was no qualitative distinction between the human and simian mind, but a distinction only of degree.

Another of my intimate friends, named Edwin Selden, belonged to a small clique of freshmen who gathered themselves about an Anglo-Catholic priest widely known under the title of Father Smythe. Besides being very devout, this coterie were ardent supporters of every Communist measure and rally, which struck me then, and still strikes me, as strangely inconsistent. I never joined them at their "Mass" or devotions, but I did once accept an invitation to go over for tea with Father Smythe. A rather handsome man in his middle forties, he impressed me, as he sat in his room of antique English furnishings, as both learned and likeable. The conversation, perhaps because of my presence, was rather matter of fact: and I confess that I was little interested in being proselytized. Selden, wiser in this respect than I, was unable to understand my indifference. I remember him asking me one time, after I had expressed complete satisfaction with being an atheist, "But haven't you any religious *feeling?*" I am afraid that I had none, nor did I care to have, because I was convinced that I could never found my faith on feeling.

Selden startled me further on another occasion by confiding to me in a whispered tone: "We hope to go over to Rome someday." Amazed, I was powerless to ask him how, if he believed in the divine authority of the Pope, he could dare to delay, and how, if he disbelieved, he could aspire to make this transfer of allegiance. Perhaps he and his companions were amassing their forces so that when they came into the Church they could drive a good bargain such as, for example, the repeal of the dogma of the Immaculate Conception. In any case, I am sure that they would have found my thinking on such matters too simple. I have quite lost track of Selden, for he left college at the end of my freshman year. I hope that he has gotten over to Rome, God bless him.

My second year in college was intellectually more fruitful than the first. My life at this point assumed a stabler and more sedentary form. I took a general course in philosophy which, introducing me to the works of Aristotle and Plato, made me perceive how much sounder was their outlook on the universe than the narrow mathematicism of Descartes and Spinoza or the sterile skepticism of Hume and Kant. The modern philosophers seemed to stultify themselves by erecting enormous epistemological difficulties at the outset. The Greeks, on the other hand, without neglecting the problem of knowledge, got much further in solving the problem of being.

From Aristotle, whom I studied more intensively in the following year, I acquired a new and far deeper concept of reality. His reasoning forced me to recognize that things are something more than hard atoms or bouncing electrons; that their natures consist less in their underlying matter than in the forms in which that matter is clothed and in the ends to which they are adapted. Matter as such, I came to understand, is passive; it can have no sensible existence and can effect nothing whatever unless it be formed, or patterned, in a certain way. In the light of this discovery I could see plainly the absurdity of declaring that the most real stage of existence was on the plane of minimum organization. On the contrary, most highly organized being was the most active and the most real. Simple electronic vibrations were but one step removed from total non-existence.

Once I had admitted the concept of degrees of reality, ranging from the most indeterminate to the most fully actuated, I was capable of distinguishing between that which is "real" and that which is "material." Matter, because it could be molded into various shapes, became associated in my thought with the potential, and form, because it was the determining principle, with the actual. I could then understand how the Supreme Being, as "Pure Act," impassible and immutable, might be altogether immaterial, and how the spiritual soul, as the "informing" principle in man, might be capable of subsisting apart from its material partner, the body.

From Aristotle, too, I learned to respect final causes. It was a tremendous step forward when I first became aware that an egg, for example, could not be completely understood by a study of its chemical composition, but that one must take account of the ideal of "chickenness" which it tended to fulfill in order to see both why the egg was constituted as it was and what it was likely to become. Thereafter I had a new notion of the meaning of philosophical explanation. If I wished to understand why a man could see, for example, I was no longer content with a reply which merely described the retina. I demanded to be informed of the purpose of sight. Ultimately the notion of purpose, or design, in my philosophy was to have its fruition in the Christian concept of Providence; but that development comes later in this narrative.

The most important influence of Aristotle on my philosophic outlook was that he gave me a totally new conception of the relation between thought and the extra-mental world. Before reading Aristotle I had been haunted by the impression that the mind's perceptions were insuperably subjective and distorted, and that extra-mental reality was something hard, unfriendly, and impenetrable. When one designated an object as round, or flat, or whatever, I considered that this was a convenient but rather careless way of describing a mental reaction, which might be a very inaccurate representation of the *Ding an sich*. At best, the predicates of roundness and flatness seemed to be tenuous hypotheses about objective realities, likely to be upset at any moment by a new discovery of Einstein.

Aristotle convinced me that the outer world was not so unattainable to the senses and the mind. He restored my confidence in the evidence of the senses by demonstrating that they were inherently susceptible of receiving sensible impressions, that their nature was to be not prison bars but windows of the soul. Reason likewise, I learned from Aristotle, was not a quality which served merely to make man a misfit in an irrational universe. It was, on the contrary, the strongest link between the soul and the outer world, being an integral part of the economy of nature and attuned to the natural law which governed the universe. So extreme had been my previous distrust of reason that even the law of contradiction, as expounded by Aristotle, came to me as a startling revelation. It had never occurred to me before that that which could be shown absurd in logic must *ipso facto* be ontologically impossible.

From the vantage point of these discoveries, I appreciated for the first time in its manifold implications the truth that rational distinctions must necessarily correspond to diversities in fact. From this it followed that the ordered universe of philosophical abstraction was not an artificial one. The chaotic world in which I had been living yielded place to the hierarchic universe of Aristotle. Reality appeared to be stratified on the progressive planes of lifeless matter, vegetable growth, then animal and finally human life (of what came higher in the scale I had as yet no definite intimation).

On apprehending the dignity of reason and its true relation to reality I all at once felt at home in the universe. It is impossible for me to exaggerate the sense of joy and freedom which came from this discovery. I soon found myself reading avidly the modern Aristotelians—Catholic authors such as Jacques Maritain and Etienne Gilson—and adhering to the logic of their doctrine with a fervor which I could hardly today recapture.

If Aristotle persuaded me that the abstractions of reason reflected the structure of reality, Plato, whom I studied concurrently, took me one step further. He convinced me that moral values had an objective basis. My previous opinions in the field of ethics had rested on the assumption that to be virtuous was merely to abide by certain conventions, or canons of behavior, representative of the collective desires of the community. Our ideas of justice, I would have said, were nothing more than a reflection of the subjective desires of particular groups of men. The moral law, even if binding, was neither stable nor universal. Its frontiers were forever shifting and uncertain. Other desires, I argued, other morals. The idea of virtue, thus conceived, held little attraction for me. I could see nothing noble or inspiring in making oneself a pliant instrument of the aspirations of others, however glorious society might wish to make subservience appear. An action which was esthetically correct was more appealing to me than one which was morally sound.

In my esthetic theories, on the other hand, I was already half a Platonist. I accepted the existence of objective standards of beauty. I was thoroughly familiar with that specious line of argument which represented the sense of beauty as a mere psychological reaction of the individual when confronted with certain phenomena which in themselves were neither beautiful nor ugly. That you or I—so ran the argument — should be thrilled by certain combinations of noises did not prove that those noises had anything particularly commendable in themselves, or that there was any justification for requiring others to have the same reaction as ourselves. Such esthetic relativism I utterly rejected, refuting its contentions by an analysis of the "creative" process. The artist, I observed, aimed ever to embody in lasting form the ideal which, by a mysterious process, sprang up within his soul. At the moment of his labors he was, commonly enough, rapt in the vision of beauty which he beheld and virtually unconscious of any potential audience. That others later enjoyed and praised his work was proof, not of the artist's intent to entertain, but of the intrinsic merit of his work.

Often, to be sure, great masterpieces had passed unrecognized. That did not, however, detract from their inherent excellence. I could not concede that the artist must cater to the public demand, or that his works should be judged according to their popular acceptance. To arraign them before the fickle court of public acclaim was in effect to set aside the esthetic law and to make a tyrant of the popular taste, which might itself be either good or bad. My own view was that art was governed by a logic of its own (different from the logic of abstract deduction), and that the critic must be schooled in the exacting science of esthetics before he could judge competently about the laws of beauty.

Beauty I considered as something supreme and absolute. Its purpose was fulfilled in its very nature. "A poem," as both Mallarmé and MacLeish had said, "must not mean but be." An ultimate value, beauty was to be sought for itself alone and not for any ulterior end. Self-sufficient, it must not tend toward anything beyond. A poem or play which attempted to inculcate some doctrine or which impelled one to adopt some course of action was, as art, impure. Didacticism was to be accounted a defect. A perfect work of beauty, I maintained, did not even elicit a state of emotion. Beauty was quieting, and its place above laughter and tears. One did not stand weeping in the Louvre, or go home from the *Alcestis* tearing one's hair. The essential note of the vision of beauty was peace, a vibrant peace charged with life and tension, a tranquillity born of the marriage of ecstasy and law.

On becoming acquainted with Plato's Idea of the Good I instantly recognized in it something closely akin to my own intuition of Beauty, transposed to the higher plane of the invisible. If my Beauty was a foretaste of heaven, so too was Plato's Good. Both were self-contained and supreme; each was to be sought for its own sake. Every experience of happiness, said Plato, is to some degree a realization of the Good. A partial attainment, I would have had it, of the beautiful.

Indeed Plato himself explicitly affirmed that the Good and the Beautiful were but one substance taken under different aspects. They were nominally distinct, but really identical, notes of an entity which in itself was unitary and indivisible. With reference to material substances Beauty, Truth and Goodness were but three designations for the same condition—conformity with the ideal pattern laid up in heaven. Beauty, in Plato's philosophy, was not merely that which induced a pleasurable sensation. It was objective excellence, insofar as it elicited acquiescence. That which pleased the senses was but the appearance of beauty. That which thrilled the intellectual vision was beauty itself. Wherever virtue or truth could be found, there beauty was also. Ugliness, conversely, was merely another name for deformity. Nothing untrue to the "forms" of nature could be either beautiful or metaphysically good.

The metaphysical good, for any particular thing, was the most perfect state of its development and internal order. Every action, organ, or object, in Plato's teaching, was to be considered good or evil according to the extent to which it fulfilled the law of its being, or, in his own terms, resembled its eternal Idea. The eye, by this criterion, is good if it sees well, the mind if it thinks well, the seamster if he sews well, the philosopher if he is wise, and the ruler if he is just.

The moral good, in the Platonic system, was that in human action which tended to realize the metaphysical good. For a man to be virtuous, then, he had only to give full scope and development to the various powers of his complex nature, with due observance to their mutual relations of authority and dependence. Pre-eminence belonged to the faculty of reason, the "eye of the soul," which discerned what was to be sought and what avoided.

The Platonic ideal of virtue had enormous consequences in my personal philosophy. Indeed it supplanted the ideal of sensible beauty as the value which I regarded as ultimate. I had previously, it now seemed, been groping after mere shadows of beauty; the senses had held in my life the position which rightfully belonged to reason. To allow concupiscence, or the desire for human esteem, or any other motive, to cause one to transgress the law governing one's own nature now appeared to me as both unintelligent and immoral. The sovereign faculty of reason alone possessed the vision of ends required for right action. Any course of action which tended to dethrone that faculty or to render the will incapable of mastering the appetites, was, I perceived, intrinsically evil. I therefore determined to spare no effort in introducing order within the inner kingdom of my soul. To succeed in life was, I now considered, to establish reason and justice in joint monarchy in one's personal life. Thus far had I progressed from the dictum of Pater which I have quoted above.

Plato's concept of virtue, unlike my previous notions of morality, was not applicable solely to the interrelations between man and man in society. Its jurisdiction over human action was unlimited and all-embracing. For the metaphysical good, upon which Plato founded his moral system, was identified with every degree and kind of excellence, and therefore coextensive with reality itself. According to Plato, the good was that which all mankind, and indeed the whole of nature, sought but to know, to love, and to imitate. Confronted by the problem of explaining why men, although so motivated, commonly pursued mere shadows rather than the substance of the good, Plato was obliged to posit the existence of some original catastrophe which had darkened the human intellect to the point where mere shadows were mistaken for realities. Thus, by rational inference, he arrived at something analogous to the doctrine of the Fall of Man, although he failed to perceive that (as Revelation teaches) that Fall has left its mark upon the human will as well as upon the intelligence. The function of philosophy, as Plato interpreted it, was but to remove the cloud of darkness which obscured man's vision of the Good. Merely to know perfection, he believed, was already to love it and to seek to realize it in the world.

In addition to being supreme and all-embracing, the Platonic ideal of virtue (which now became my own) was natural, objective and universal. Founded solidly upon the structure of reality, the moral law was to be reckoned not as a mere matter of opinion but as the object of a genuine science. Perceiving that the nature of the good was independent of the flux of human desires, Plato by-passed at once the sterile dichotomies of egoism *versus* altruism and pain *versus* pleasure which are responsible for the futility of so many ethical discussions. The moral law to which he pointed claimed allegiance both in Athens and New York, in the polar regions and in the tropics, whether in the bustle of the market-place, in the privacy of the home, or in the solitude of a desert island. No matter what one's surroundings, Plato insisted, the qualities proper to man as man remained the same. Wisdom, justice, temperance, and fortitude always and undeniably surpassed their opposites. I was unable to deny that this was so.

In order to complete the foregoing summary of the effect of Plato and Aristotle on my intellectual outlook, I have expounded certain ideas which I did not clearly grasp until the beginning, or even the middle, of my junior year in college, but which began to germinate in my mind when I first studied the writings of these ancient thinkers. Having anticipated certain subsequent developments, I must now ask the

reader to return with me to the cold, amoral
world in which, philosophically speaking, I still
found myself at the beginning of my sophomore
year—a world governed only by chance and by
the selfish actions of human persons engaged in
the cruel quest for pleasure.

The feature which dominates my entire second year at Harvard is that I then made the acquaintance of the man who first gave me a vivid
picture of the Catholic faith. His name was
Paul Doolin, and he was, through an unmerited
dispensation of Providence on my behalf, assigned as my tutor. A convert to the Catholic
faith, Doolin was about to leave his teaching position at Harvard to accept an appointment to
the faculty of the Jesuit college of Georgetown.
But God spared him for me at Harvard long
enough so that I was able to study under him
for eight months.

A dynamic, black-haired, blue-eyed Irishman,
Paul Doolin recaptured in his imagination and
reincarnated in his person the spirit of the
Middle Ages. Always dramatic, forceful, and
sudden in his speech, his technique was to persuade not so much by arguing as by amazing.
He could always find a single phrase or observation which went to the absolute root of the

matter at hand. He had a marvelous gift for presenting his ideas in concrete terms, without becoming involved in vaporous abstractions, and every word which he spoke was a living expression of his own rich philosophy. His statements were not impartial observations, they were intense personal convictions.

His scheme of values, which seemed a little incongruous in his age and surroundings, was completely at odds with the spirit of the times, at least at Harvard. Doolin was the implacable enemy of materialism, utilitarianism, humanitarianism, pacifism and sentimentality in every form. When asked one time what he would do if given a million dollars, he replied, in his terse, vigorous speech, "Send tanks to Franco." Thus by a single phrase he characteristically opposed himself, not with logic but with his very person, to both the "liberal" interventionists and the pacifist non-interventionists who took sides in nearly every discussion of American foreign policy at the time.

A man cast in the heroic mold, a crusader born out of time, Doolin went to extremes in his denunciation of the prevalent errors. His unsparing mockery extended to sweeping condemnations of whole ages, classes, nations, and races, and occasionally gave rise to misinterpretations. Some considered him an anti-Semite and some a fascist, but both these accusations were unjust.

As a deep Christian Doolin had an abiding love for all mankind and perhaps specially for the race of Our Lord. His vociferous indignation against the majority of Jews—of whom Marx and Freud were to his mind the aptest symbols—was dogmatic and moral, and ought not to be confused with personal spite or vulgar prejudice.

Doolin's political views were poles apart from fascism. An authoritarian and a legitimist in the French school, he was on principle, I imagine, an adherent of limited monarchy. He taught a brilliant course in the history of France from the Fifteenth to the Eighteenth Century, the essential thesis of which was to attribute the calamity of the French Revolution to the unscrupulous absolutism of Richelieu and Louis XIV, combined with the bad philosophy of the so-called Enlightenment. A profound student of the history of political thought, Doolin was convinced that that science had died with the age of Jean Bodin and Saint Robert Bellarmine. For modern liberalism he had only the greatest contempt. The Eighteenth Century he dismissed as an "age without political thought," referring to that great constitutional historian, Charles Homer McIlwaine, as the author of this perspicacious observation. With his deep sense of the importance of spiritual values, Doolin could not countenance the view of Locke and Montesquieu that the State should concern itself only with the distribution of material things. Like the philosophers of the ancient world, he maintained that the State should take an active part in securing the welfare of souls as well as of bodies. The greatest offense against the State, he would quote from Plato's *Laws,* is to teach error. In Hitler he saw a not untoward revolt against the materialism which had dominated the political thought of the two preceding centuries. Yet he despised most of the canons of National Socialism. The doctrine of the *raison d'état* and the very name of Machiavelli were to him anathema.

Many times I had occasion to discuss with Doolin questions of literature. He had no use, I found, for the seductions of lyric poetry, a form of writing which he characterized, Platonically, as a vain and repulsive display of private sentiment, with special attention to the emotion of self-pity. When I professed a certain admira-

tion for Shakespeare he turned me sharply
aside by quoting Milton's criticism:

> . . . sweetest Shakespear fancies childe,
> Warble his native Wood-notes wilde.

To Doolin, Milton's name was magic. More
than any other poet, Milton exemplified for
him the incomparable superiority of epic over
lyric poetry. For all his unsavory connections
with the policies of the Protectorate and with
Cromwell's dark vengeance on the Irish Catholics, Milton was Doolin's ideal of lofty zeal, integrity, and spiritual grandeur.

While the still morn went out with sandals grey

. . . he would quote reverently, adding with a
    growl,
"That takes imagination!"

The reason behind Doolin's distaste for lyric
poetry was fundamentally a moral one. Lyric-
ism, he recognized, was radically sensate and
emotional, as opposed to epic or dramatic
poetry, which is more commonly what sociolo-
gists are wont to label "ideate." Having personally experienced the captivating power of the
goddess of beauty, Doolin had formed a deep
distrust for the estheticism of the senses. In his

Platonic philosophy beauty held a place of honor, provided, however, that it was united with the good. True beauty, in his opinion, must serve to strengthen the moral faculty rather than to stimulate the concupiscent powers of the soul.

To put a label on his philosophy, one might call Doolin a Platonist, or perhaps better an Augustinian. Like the great Carthaginian Bishop of ancient times, Doolin had come to Christianity and to the Catholic Church from a species of Platonism, and particularly from the doctrine of the *Symposium* that love is a force which tends naturally upward toward the divine. Plato, he would say flatly, was very close to Christ.

Doolin's profound grasp and appreciation of the Platonic doctrine of love was, like so many of his intuitions, based on his individual experience. His own approach to Christianity had undoubtedly been wrought through love—as I suspect is the case with all conversions. And love was the great force in Doolin's character which gave him his undeniable power and stature.

Few, however, perceived that this was so. Disdainful of sentimentality, Doolin was methodically reticent and ever at pains to conceal

his more tender feelings behind a wall of gruff-
ness. "He doesn't wear his heart on his sleeve,"
he would say when he wished to compliment
someone. The compliment applied admirably
to himself. The books which Doolin wrote were
so impressive an assemblage of facts and deduc-
tions, marshalled with such Euclidian precision,
that they read like a lawyer's brief or a treatise
on logic. In his lectures, likewise, he studiously
avoided all oratory: he would read with lowered
chin from little scraps of paper in a monotonous
tone of voice. The more superficial students,
looking for outward flourish rather than substance, were disappointed or even bored.

I studied under Professor Doolin, as I have
said, for only eight months, and was at the time
deeply intrenched in the false philosophy which
I have described in the first pages of this essay.
I was struck principally by the originality of
Doolin's opinions. They were a stimulating contrast to all that I had ever heard. Nearly three
years were to pass before I found my way into
the Catholic Church, but throughout that
period the teaching of Paul Doolin was to serve
me as a guide and reference point. At the time
of hearing it, I was not yet ready to receive

Doolin's doctrine, but I treasured it up in the garners of my memory, and drew abundantly therefrom in the years that followed. The reasoning behind some of his sudden and abrupt sentences did not become clear to me until long afterward, but their very obscurity served to make one think, for everything that Doolin said fell into an ultimate pattern. None of his remarks was casual or flippant.

The great importance which Doolin's teaching had for my intellectual development is attributable to the gradual crumbling of my materialist philosophy which began in my sophomore year. I would not have been so receptive to the ideas which I found expressed in the imperishable writings of Plato and Aristotle and in the arresting speech of Paul Doolin except that the inward rottenness of my own philosophy was becoming desperately obvious.

Increasingly I was forced to acknowledge that a life based consistently on the pursuit of pleasure could not be rich either in achievement or in happiness.

An admirer always of the heritage of civilization, I became sadly aware that few of the great achievements of mankind could have been wrought if their authors had been motivated by mere considerations of advantage. The most magnificent works of human architecture were temples and churches, erected for the praise and honor of God. The masterpieces of art which I esteemed were principally religious in character, having as their aim to instruct the faithful, to remind them of their various relationships to God, and to help them to pray rightly to Him and to His saints. When art, in the later Renaissance, became secularized, esthetic delight being made supreme, decadence simultaneously set in. The great voyages of discovery, too, were many of them undertaken with the object of bringing the Christian faith to those who still languished in heathen ignorance. The world-shaking wars of conquest of all ages had been fought, not for the personal satisfaction of the soldiers, but for king, for country and for God.

Often, to be sure, actors had risen to eminence on the stage of life who sought no higher prize than personal wealth or fame or power. But to that extent they had been deluded. They failed to reap the harvest which they sowed, or, like the empire builders who devoted their lives to the amassing of material treasure, they awoke to find themselves grown old and their hoard but dust and ashes in their hands. They would have done better, according to their own standards, to have shortened the arm of their ambition and to have dwelt, like Lucretius or Spinoza, in the peace of a narrow garden.

Indeed my own state of mind was such that I questioned whether they had done well to live at all. The amount of personal pleasure which this world could afford did not seem great enough to compensate for all its loneliness and tears. Private enjoyment was not an adequate guerdon to justify the heartache and the pain. The temptation, therefore, was terribly insistent to extract every drop of pleasure within immediate reach, and then put a term to this dreary existence. I might have done as much except that my thought was developing along new lines.

Love, I perceived, was the strongest impulse of the human heart, yet in my philosophy it held no place. The fatal defect of my outlook in life, oriented as it was toward the pursuit of pleasure, was that it thwarted the most basic human instincts, to love, to labor and to serve. Hence the shallowness and misery of my existence, which daily threatened to become intolerable. My philosophy failed me because it was not big enough to contain the human, let alone the heroic. By an odd paradox, I noted, man could find no joy unless he sought it not, unless he lived by love, which "seeketh not her own." Was there, I asked, some other good, above and apart from human enjoyment, capable of eliciting the boundless resources of devotion, loyalty and fortitude which lay dormant in the soul? Was there some end sufficiently exalted to justify great undertakings and to deploy in all their splendor the faculties of mind and character with which man is endowed?

Many of my friends, I observed, were driven by this very need of finding some ideal, transcending personal pleasure, to which they could consecrate their lives. With more emotion than logic they prostrated themselves before the various human ideals which were in vogue. Some of them found satisfaction in devoting their energies to the progress of mankind, which they interpreted as the liberation of the toiling masses from the chains of capitalistic greed. Lacking religion, they bowed down to the imposing

eschatology[1] of Marx, which, while neatly ac-
counting for the all too evident misery of man,
yet ministered to that hope for something better
which ever burns within the human breast.
While I envied the strength of their conviction
and of their devotion, I considered the doctrines
of these self-styled liberals both false and dangerous. In my heart I knew that the philosophy
of Marx was wrong, because it took its departure from a false psychology. Having set out with
an erroneous view of the human spirit—in effect, the classic hypothesis of economic man—
Marx could never I knew, make a correct analysis of the operations of that spirit in history or
prescribe accurately the form which society
should finally assume.

The psychology of the fascists, who had a
very mediocré following at Harvard, impressed
me as being somewhat sounder because it gave
a place for love and sacrifice. But fascism's tech-
niques of mob action, its dogmas of race and
blood, and, above all, its exaltation of the State

---

[1] The word eschatology may, I think, be used advisedly
of a system which conceives of history as a monstrous
dialectic of clashing interests tending constantly toward
the final merger of the individual with the collective
will, and looks toward the ultimate disappearance of
caste rivalries in the static heaven of a classless society.

as the absolute good, were to me unacceptable. I remained untouched in my belief that the State was made for man, not man for the State.

Democracy, which I had previously assumed to be an unqualified blessing, began to appear under a less glistening aspect. By this I do not mean that I denied its purposes. I have always believed that the proper end of the State is to secure the well-being of all the people. But I refer to Democracy as an ideology, as the crude Nineteenth Century doctrine, nowhere completely put into practice, that the opinions and aspirations of the majority should determine the policies and actions of the State. That such government from below was a positive good I could not concede. At times, to be sure, it might be a necessary measure to protect the populace against the selfishness of a corrupt ruling class, but, ideally at least, the State should serve some higher purpose than to conform to the whims and illusions of the masses. Government, as I saw it, was a science having as its end the bodily and spiritual welfare of the whole community. Like other sciences, it required of its practitioners that they be loyal to its own object. Unbridled self-interest, in rulers as in private citizens, was a vice to be guarded against. But, and again like other sciences, government should be practiced by those who had the necessary learning and experience. In this I likened it to law and medicine. The argument that civil government, since it affected all, was everybody's business, impressed me little. Everyone, I replied, is interested in the good practice of medicine, but no one has seriously proposed that the manner of performing appendectomies should be made the object of a general referendum, or that M.D. degrees should be accorded by popular suffrage.

These political considerations may appear somewhat out of place in this essay, but I regard them as important in my religious development. In the first place, a little careful thought about such matters helped me to get over the juvenile notion that the individual must be the judge of all things. I saw that in questions of state, it was necessary to submit to the authority of qualified arbiters. I soon found myself at odds with those liberalistic forces, so prevalent at Harvard at the time, which were constantly making the "authoritarian" Catholic Church the butt of their invective. I, by contrast, became increasingly disposed to accept authority, not only in politics, but also in faith and morals.

I learned, also, the futility of trying to confer upon political ideologies that absolute loyalty which is paid to religious faith. I came to the view, which has remained with me ever since, that no particular form of government is a universal and unqualified good. Monarchies, oligarchies, and democracies—all are capable of being either efficient or corrupt. Systems of government, after all, are only so many methods of securing benefits to the governed. Much depends on what benefits are to be sought, for no one system is appropriate to every end. A society organized for war (for example, an army) should be differently constituted than a society consecrated to the blessings of peace. The particular social conditions must also be taken into account. Even the fondest zealots of democracy seemed to admit this by occasionally asserting that not all societies are "ripe" for self-government. To my mind, one of the great lessons of history was that royal and aristocratic societies, and even benevolent dictatorships, have at various times served to establish and maintain in a satisfactory degree the order, prosperity and liberty which most men lawfully desire. I could not, then, enroll myself under the banner of any particular political apostolate, and I distrusted the easy fanaticism with which some of my friends embraced certain ideals of government as if they were the sole font of salvation. They neglected to allow for diversities of social conditions and to consider seriously the ends for which governments are instituted. The purposes of human government, I perceived, were dependent on the purposes of human life. The latter must be discovered before the former could be intelligently discussed.

In my effort, then, to find some political ideal to which the whole man could be unreservedly dedicated, I was defeated. I was thrown back squarely on the moral and religious problem, which I had sought to avoid. The question, what is the final end of man, was abstruse and therefore unpleasant. But it called implacably for an answer. "Personal pleasure" I had already found inadequate as a goal. To erect in its place some abstract *summum bonum* was easy. Too easy, because, unless more positive content were given to that formula, it did not answer either the moral problem or the personal need. To say, the absolute good is the end in view of which all my actions must be ordered, did not in itself establish any standard of conduct. Nor did the "absolute good", because of its abstract and impersonal nature, suffice to establish an adequate object on which to fix the energies of love, the impetus to serve and sacrifice, which were inescapably present in man.

In the darkness of my inner world the highest human instincts were confronted with a vacuum. Into that vacuum stepped the grace of God. The barren desolation of my materialist philosophy, its utter falseness and my humiliation at discovering it so, gave God His chance. The very extremeness of my error made conversion easier. Perhaps if I had had more specious beliefs and affections—some human idealism or some earthly loyalty— I might have been less willing to accept God's offering of Himself.

This offering occurred, suddenly and quite unexpectedly, on one grey February afternoon like many another. I was in Widener Library poring over a chapter of the *De civitate Dei* which had been assigned as reading in one of my courses in medieval history. On an impluse I closed the book; I was irresistibly prompted to go out into the open air. It was a bleak rainy day, rather warm for the time of year. The

slush of melting snow formed a deep mud along
the banks of the River Charles, which I followed down toward Boston. I enjoyed the cool
rain in my face and the melancholy of the scene.
As I wandered aimlessly, something impelled
me to look contemplatively at a young tree.
On its frail, supple branches were young buds
attending eagerly the spring which was at hand.
While my eye rested on them the thought came
to me suddenly, with all the strength and novelty of a revelation, that these little buds in their
innocence and meekness followed a rule, a law
of which I as yet knew nothing. How could it
be, I asked, that this delicate tree sprang up
and developed and that all the enormous com-
plexity of its cellular operations combined together to make it grow erectly and bring forth
leaves and blossoms? The answer, the trite
answer of the schools, was new to me: that its
actions were ordered to an end by the only
power capable of adapting means to ends—
intelligence—and that the very fact that this
intelligence worked toward an end implied
purposiveness—in other words, a will. It was
useless, then, to dismiss these phenomena by
obscurantist talk about a mysterious force called
"Nature." The "nature" which was respon-

sible for these events was distinguished by the possession of intellect and will, and intellect plus will makes personality. Mind, then, not matter, was at the origin of all things. Or rather not so much the "mind" of Anaxagoras as a Person of Whom I had had no previous intuition.

Nor were the operations of this Person confined to flowers and foliage. The harmonious motions of the stars, the distribution of the elements, and the obedience of matter to fixed laws were manifestations of the same will and plan. Looking, then, into myself, I beheld energies coursing through the human person, the greater part of them beyond the realm of consciousness, tending constantly to preserve, to nourish, and to restore the weary body and soul. These forces were not of our own making, these operations not established by ourselves. Yet they had from their inception a legitimacy which was conferred upon them by Another—the same as Him Who moved the stars and made the lilacs bloom.

If, then, the very energies of growth and healing in the human body were hedged with sacredness, was it not monstrous that we, incapable of creating a hair, should undertake to dispose of our whole being, heedless of its appointed end? One had but to attend closely to the movements of the soul, when free from passion and from the self-induced blindness of perversity, to sense the marvelous harmony of all its tendencies, working in unison for the fulfillment in us of the divine purpose. Most of all was this true, as Plato and Aristotle had observed, of the spiritual faculties. The mind, as they had remarked, is naturally adapted toward knowledge and tends, unless obstructed, toward the apprehension of truth. The will, analogously, ever seeks the good and finds its fulfillment in ordering the lower parts of the soul according to the vision of the good which it beholds. To frustrate these tendencies, more native to us than ourselves, in a frenzied search for some arbitrary goal of our own choosing appeared in an unmistakable light to be blasphemous infraction of an eternal canon. Something sacred, I sensed, is violated, and a priceless opportunity irrevocably lost, when the mind is steeped in drunkenness and the will deprived of its energy, when lust for pleasure uses the mind as its instrument and debauches the effeminate will.

A glance at that great governing will and intellect which had given to all nature, the wide universe, its origin and end was a strong potion, awaking energies not easily harnessed or turned back. As I turned home that evening, the darkness closing round, I was conscious that I had discovered something which would introduce me to a new life, set off by a sharp hiatus from the past.

That night, for the first time in years, I prayed. I knelt down in the chill blackness at my bedside, as my mother had taught me to do when I was a little boy, and attempted to raise my heart and mind toward Him of Whose presence and power I had become so unexpectedly aware. I recited the Our Father. The words came slowly, and I had to make many new starts before the whole prayer unfolded itself in my mind. Our Father Who art in Heaven. Hallowed be Thy name. Thy will be done on earth, as it is in heaven . . .

My first religious intimations, as the reader will observe, took on a Christian aspect. This Being Whom I perceived as the cause and consummation of the universe, the Alpha and Omega of all creation, was unmistakably the God of Christianity. He had nothing in common with the pagan myths of Zeus, of Thor, or of Brahma, about which I had read. He was not merely the abstract Good or Beautiful, nor was He the isolated Pure Act of Aristotle. He was Our Father Who had made us; He had a will which was done in heaven, but which we, with our selfish and perverse designs, were capable of frustrating, or at least of accomplishing in an unbefitting way.

At this point in my intellectual development —we have now arrived at the middle of my junior year in college—I had discovered several fundamental verities about the universe which served as the basis for a positive natural religion. In the first place, Plato had convinced me that good and evil were categories corresponding to objective realities, rather than mere fictions of the human mind. The Christian conception of God had perfected this Platonic intuition and infused it with a fresh vitality. As a result I saw beyond question that deliberately to obstruct the divine will, as manifested in nature, was absolutely and incontrovertibly evil. Conversely, to adhere to the divine purpose was, by objective and indubitable standards, good. I had, of course, no notion of the divine law except a natural one. I could see that the various organs of the body and soul had been established for definite ends. This fact was enough to establish the basic premise that moral values were something more than mere illusions.

Secondly, I saw that nothing was more to be done than the good, since the good, in its moral signification, is defined as that which ought to be done. In this conception, inchoate though it was, lay tremendous possibilities of development. Here at last was a Cause to which the entire man could be dedicated and a sure means of escaping the woeful emptiness of a life based merely on the avoidance of pain. Pleasure might in some way be related to the good—I was not to understand how until later—but I could be certain at least that the two were not identical. I saw the rectitude of Plato's view that he would rather be cast eternally into a pit in chains than commit an injustice. With pride I made that view my own.

But—and this is the specifically theistic element in my philosophy at the time—the good which I held to be supreme and worthy of all man's devotion was not an abstract ideal. It was a personal will, throbbing through the whole universe as the force which had created it, the power which sustained it in existence, and the goal toward which it tended. The moral good was merely an aspect of the Adorable Will of God. No abstract notion of the good could impress me as ultimate. The good was a value, and value implied appreciation, which is a function of personality. The good, conceived in personal terms, was capable of being made the object of loyalty and personal devotion. Dimly I saw that personality as such was higher than any lifeless thing, and that to serve or worship anything, be it concrete or abstract, which lacked intellect and volition, was to debase oneself and to desecrate the dignity of one's own being.

In the possession of this tripartite creed, made up of the existence of the moral law, its supremacy, and its relation to the will of God, I found a degree and quality of happiness which I had never before thought possible. The values which it established precluded any radical pessimism. Within its framework one could discover ends in terms of which one's actions could be purposively coordinated. Far as I was from the Catholic faith, the road now was a straight one. And philosophy had put me on that road.

I do not claim that I was or am or ever will be a philosopher in the sense of an expert on metaphysical questions. But in another sense anyone who stops to wonder what he should do or why he does that which he does must be a philosopher. He must formulate some guiding principles in terms of which he can make practical decisions. He must seek out the premises implied in his own actions and see to it that they are mutually consistent and theoretically sound.

Many persons pretend that philosophy is a dull study and one which has no relation to practical life. For me it has never been so. It was terribly clear to me from the beginning that I could not do anything—whether to help a friend in trouble, to eat a meal, or even to take a breath—without running the risk of being asked by some Socrates, Why? What is the principle by which you justify this action? Does it ultimately tend to bring about that which you deem to be worth while? These questions haunted me, and I could have no peace until they had been answered. I would rather not act at all than act with the knowledge that I might better be doing nothing or doing the very opposite.

The man who refuses to face the philosophic problem is like a traveler in the night who will not take the time to decide where he is going because he is too much in a hurry to be on his way. He hastens first in one direction, then in the other, repeatedly striking his foot against cobble stones and stumbling in ruts, without approaching any nearer to his destination because he does not know whither he is bound. He becomes a slave to irrational impulses which incline him now this way and now that. Eventually he resolves that he will follow the crowd, but he has no way of telling whether they are proceeding to the same destination or whether they know where it is located. They disagree among themselves and he listens to their confused, discordant counsels. Finally he determines to follow the man who speaks in the loudest, most emphatic tones. When he has been led to one of those dead ends where error ends in impossibility he finds out to his grief that the ignorant prophet whom he had chosen to follow was one of those hireling leaders who speak with conviction in order to gratify a personal passion for having others follow them.

The general refusal of mankind to attempt to answer the questions raised by Socrates is perhaps the most dangerous folly in an age when folly seems to reign. The opinion that blind appetite could furnish a sufficient guide for action led to the general undermining of democracy. The consequent willingness of men to listen to any voice which spoke with accents of authority has permitted the establishment of unprecedented tyrannies. Man can not with impunity continue to ignore philosophy. Happily, the actions of most of us are still superior to our philosophy. We are heirs to many of the conventions of Christianity, but most of us have put aside the articles of its creed. Ultimately, unless we restore our belief in God and our understanding of the moral law, the remainder of our Christian heritage will disintegrate. We will be left with naught but naked, savage cruelty. It is an ominous sign that great bodies of supposedly Christian persons have lately been seduced by myths of race and blood. And it is not impossible that the future holds yet darker errors.

The world needs philosophy, just as I needed it. Through a little elementary thinking about the purposes of our existence and the nature of the universe in which we live, we can prop up with reason the crumbling structure of our culture. If thought alone can not bring us back to the faith of our ancestors, God grant that it may at least restore us to the level of ancient

civilization and thus serve to stem the tidal
wave of barbarism which threatens to engulf us.

PART II

Never, since the eventful day which I have described, have I doubted the existence of an all-good and omnipotent God. Proofs there were, and I had read them in the philosophy books. The proofs served to confirm and to clarify, but they could not have produced in its fulness my own conviction of the existence of God. All the proofs of God, precisely because they were proofs of something unseen, depended on the principle of sufficient reason. This principle, however well established, somehow failed to carry conviction to my mind. Certain in itself, it was not certain to me. Every rational demonstration seemed to leave room for just a particle of skepticism, which, as a result of man's natural disinclination to commit himself, could be turned to enormous account. My own acceptance of the existence of God rested on something more like an intuition. It was as though I had seen, at least for an instant, the divine power at work, infusing the whole universe with goodness and being. This intuition was by no means mystical, but it was a personal experience, and as such I find it partly incommunicable. I recorded it as best I can for whatever autobiographical interest it may have.

My path from this point to the Catholic

Church was straight, as I have said, but it was long and steep. I did not become a Catholic until nearly two years later, after having begun my course at law school. My entire religious background was Protestant. My family on both sides had been Presbyterians for generations, and not one of my closer friends was a believing Catholic. In my existing environment I was almost completely isolated from Catholic doctrine, and a certain reticence, which I have never overcome, about discussing religious subjects, made it unthinkable at the time for me to enter a Catholic rectory for consultation with a priest. My religious intimations were at once too personal and too confused for vocal expression. The only conceptions which I had of the Catholic religion were those drawn from the teaching of Paul Doolin and a few scattered notions which I had gathered from my studies in medieval history.

It is not surprising, therefore, that I first thought of religion in Protestant terms.

The essential point is that I did think of religion. Indeed, in the time that was my own, I thought of almost nothing else. There was no question in my mind but that the only good worthy of the name was the praise and service of Almighty God. And I knew of no joy comparable with that of increasing one's understanding of the nature and operations of the Divine personality in Whom all goodness and truth and being had their source. "As the hart panteth after the waterbrooks, so panteth my soul after the Lord." That quotation could serve as the caption for the next two years of my life.

Principally I found enlightenment concerning the Divine personality in the Gospels. I made it a rule—and one which I have found it harder to break than to keep—that every night, no matter how busy I might be, I would read at least one chapter from the New Testament. I kept up this custom for the next two years, never omitting a night when it was possible for me to observe my rule.

The words of Our Lord, as recorded in the Gospels, rang with undeniable truth, but never more so, to my mind, than when He insisted, as He repeatedly did, on the knowledge and love of God as the only things that mattered. Suffering and persecution, He reiterated, were positive blessings when endured for His sake. Religion was the pearl of great price, the water which alone could wholly quench our thirst;

and He was the way, the truth and the life. Far more clearly than any man He taught that blessedness, not pleasure, should be the object of our lives. This was the doctrine for which I had been searching, and I accepted it with joy.

Who was this Teacher, or better this Lover, Who could not be restrained from giving until the last drop of blood had left His martyred body? Who was He, that He bade us so insistently to follow Him, begged to refresh us with His doctrine and to make us partakers of His joy? Was He, as He claimed, God and the Son of God?

After acquainting myself a little with the Gospels, I could have no patience with those modern writers and speakers who were incessantly trying to water down His "hard" doctrine, and to represent Christ Himself as a mild, tolerant and ever gentle moralist. I was impressed by His unsparing rage against the Pharisees and by His use of physical violence to cleanse the Temple from the moneychangers. I saw that He was a man Whom one could hate tremendously, as most of His contemporaries did hate Him, for what they took to be his bad manners and extravagant ideas. The thought occurred to me that most of those who attempted to make Christ seem so moderate and "respectable" would have hated and feared Him had they known Him as He was.

Christ, as He appeared in the Scriptures, was not primarily a moralist. For conduct as such He cared relatively little; love and faith He cherished above measure. His teaching took the form, not of dry aphorisms like those of Confucius or Poor Richard, but of parables charged with the poetry of life. These parables were so direct that the most unlettered could grasp their message. At the same time they were so rich in doctrine and symbolism that the most learned could not exhaust their subtle moral implications, their wealth of dogma and their deep prophetic meaning. The moralists never seemed to rise above the obvious. Christ never paused to state the obvious. He told of things no man had seen.

Nor was He merely a philosopher, another Socrates or Plotinus. They, after long inductive processes, came to tentative conclusions about the nature of God, the immortality of the soul, and the good life. Christ, Who seemed a stranger to discursive thought, spoke readily and with finality about these matters. He could use keen logic, and often did so to confute the

Scribes and Pharisees, but His knowledge of spiritual matters was direct and immediate. His doctrine, higher than that of the philosophers, did not have the same source.

But could not Christ be classed as a religious fanatic, like Mohammed for example? To compare Him with the frenzied Arab epileptic was outright blasphemy. His judgment, unlike that of the fanatics, was always calm and clear, and His perception of His environment complete and penetrating. His doctrine, moreover, was thoroughly consistent with itself and with the facts of nature. When the philosophers later made it their study they found that the Christian faith enabled them to see clearly what Plato and Aristotle had hesitantly inferred. Once Christ had lived, Western philosophy could never be the same again. Mohammed had had no comparable influence on Arabic philosophy.

Was it possible, then, that Christ was more than a man? I investigated the arguments for His divinity, and found them no less cogent for being conventional. First, there was an embarrassing frequency of miracles in all the accounts of Christ. If He had performed any of them, He might well have performed all. He was neither a charlatan nor a fool, yet He repeatedly claimed miraculous powers, and, if the accounts had any normal degree of veracity, demonstrated that power again and again. The doctrine of the Gospels was sublime, and was indubitably a faithful account of Christ's teaching. To whom else could one accredit it? But was the view tenable that the miracles were something superadded by ignorant and credulous disciples? In Lionel Curtis's *City of God* I had read an able presentation of that thesis, but I found it unacceptable. Christ's doctrine was inseparably wedded to His miracles. Time and again He had illustrated His doctrine by His miracles and invoked His miracles as proof of His doctrine. One had to take both or neither. If, then, the Gospel accounts of Christ's doctrine were authentic—as I could not but concede—the miracles also must be accepted. Mr. Curtis, I felt, was not meeting the facts squarely. He was tailoring them to fit the frame of his own narrow rationalism.

One miracle which stood up to every test was the Resurrection. Any attempt to dismiss it as a hallucination was useless. That thousands of persons should have suffered a hallucination extending over a period of forty days was

harder to account for than the Resurrection itself. Was it, then, a clever trick of Christ or
His disciples? Nothing could have been more
unlike Christ than to masquerade as a walking
corpse in order to deceive His followers. And
nothing could have been more unlike the disciples, who had weakly denied Christ in His
Passion, than to go out and die for a myth of
their own coinage.

The most persuasive proof of all for me was
the way in which this risen Christ acted. What
literary artist could have thought up such con-
versations as Christ held when He said Mass
for the pilgrims at Emmaus ("Did not our
hearts burn within us as He spoke?"), when He
convinced the doubting Thomas, and when He
commissioned Saint Peter to feed His sheep?
In all these incidents one senses unmistakably
the personality of Christ. The very detail is evidence of a sane and honest witness. It is even
recorded that He ate broiled fish and honey-
comb. If an accomplished novelist could not
have invented all this, how could a group of
lying or demented fishermen have done so?

Further testimony of the divinity of Christ
was contained in the Prophecies. It seemed at
least a peculiar coincidence that this righteous,

wise, and powerful Person, Whose works and teaching themselves suggested that He was more than a man, should have been born, not a Greek or a Roman, but a Jew—a member of that race which had cherished from time immemorial the promise of a Messias. Still more remarkable did it appear that Jesus was conceived in the manner predicted of the Redeemer, born in the prescribed village, and that He suffered in every detail the afflictions and death foretold of the Messias.

The wicked Herod, the holy Simeon, and a handful of others were alone in recognizing the applicability of the Prophecies. The priests and Pharisees utterly misconstrued them, and so likewise did the disciples when they took scandal at His death. Yet the Scriptures were strangely accurate. How eloquently the dolorous Passion had been depicted in the Psalms: "All they that see Me laugh Me to scorn . . . They pierced My hands and My feet: they have numbered all My bones. They look and stare upon Me. They part My garments among them, and upon My vesture they cast lots." The Psalms were filled with similar predictions, and likewise the Book of Jeremias, but none had foreseen so accurately as Isaias, and in such

marvelous detail, the birth, life, and death of
Our Lord. His writings abounded in startling
prognostications: "Behold a virgin shall con-
ceive . . .," "All ye that pass by the way attend
and see . . .," "There is no beauty in Him nor
comeliness . . ." Was it not possible that in
these and other texts, unsurpassed in literary
merit, the Holy Ghost had revealed to the
ancient seers the life of Him upon Whom they
set their hopes? Indeed it seemed likely that
Christ was the promised Savior of Whom they
had written.

If the Messianic commission of Christ was at-
tested by the Prophecies, the same could equally
well be said of the Figures, in which Christ was
foreshadowed not in thought only, but in deed.
I was deeply impressed by the mysterious symbolism which penetrated the actions of Noe,
Isaac, Moses, Jonas, Melchisedech, and the
other precursors of Christ. Most apt of all the
Figures, to my mind, was the Joseph episode.
The most beloved of Jacob's sons, he arouses
the jealousy of his brothers. They equivalently
put him to death and entomb him in a pit. He
rises from the pit and goes before them into a
far country. A famine occurs, and the family
of Joseph are forced, with the humility of the

Prodigal Son, to beg sustenance from him whom they had thought to kill and who now reigns in a land of abundance. On discovering his identity, his brothers fear for their lives. He forgives them, however, and bestows upon them far more than they had dared to ask. Written many centuries before Christ's birth, the story of Joseph was a perfect parable of His death and resurrection.

Indeed, I observed, the entire Old Testament could be read as an allegory of the New. Every sacrifice offered up by the priests and patriarchs under the Old Law was an inadequate effort to accomplish in advance the Paschal sacrifice of Christ, the Lamb of God. Every aspiration to reach the Promised Land was a mystical striving to force the gates of heaven, which were to be opened by Christ. The works and sufferings of the ancient Prophets could not be properly interpreted except in terms of the coming of Him to whom their hearts incessantly went forth, "the desire of the everlasting hills."

The Messianic character of Christ's mission appeared not only in these adumbrations of His coming, but equally in the events which filled His life as He walked on earth. His personal eminence as a teacher and as a virtuous man paled to insignificance beside the vicarious role which He played as Victim and Redeemer. He was the second Adam, the progenitor of grace, and was destined, through the fruit of the Tree of the Cross, to repair the damage wrought by the first Adam in partaking of the fruit of the forbidden Tree.

Every incident in the life of Christ was intimately linked with His redemptive mission. Each of His miracles, I perceived, illustrated in a particular way His relation to the entire human species in the order of grace. When He changed the water into wine at Cana, for example, He was not merely performing a courteous service to relieve His host's embarrassment. The wine which He gave to the marriage guests was symbolic of His own Advent when the sources of prophetic wisdom seemed to have run dry. More precisely, that exquisite wine could be interpreted as signifying the Precious Blood which He was to shed for mankind on the altar of the Cross. Again, when Our Lord satisfied the hunger of the five thousand on the mountain, He mystically anticipated the immolation of His Body on Calvary, explicitly declaring at the time, "The bread that I will give is

My flesh." Similarly, when, after the Resurrection, He brought in the miraculous draft of fishes, He was not merely giving evidence of His divine power or ministering to the material needs of His disciples: He was demonstrating to Peter how great a multitude of souls He would later draw into the Church. The event must be understood in terms of the words, "Behold, I will make you fishers of men." The extraordinary strength of the net, which causes the Evangelist to remark that it did not break, is an indication of the indivisibility of the Church.

In the whole of Christ's earthly sojourn, I perceived, there is not one occurence, however trivial in appearance, which does not take on momentous proportions in terms of His capacity as Messias. Each event tends to confirm and to clarify His cosmic mission. Nothing is left to chance: a dramatic necessity presides over all. In one way or another every circumstance serves to establish more positively Christ's supernatural role as an acceptable oblation for man's sin.

Even his enemies assist Our Lord to become the protagonist of this colossal drama of reparation. The anguish and contumely which they rudely heap upon Him are the predestined lot of one who is to be offered up to the Father as an immaculate victim. The callous indifference of the enrolees who had congregated at Bethlehem excluded Our Lady from the hospitality of the inn, and brought upon Our Lord the humble circumstances of His Birth. The jealousy of Herod made Him an exile from the first moment of His childhood. The hypocrisy of the Pharisees compelled Him to live His public life as an outcast and a wanderer. The avarice of Judas, the worldliness of Pontius Pilate, and the savage inconstancy of the populace prepared His mournful Passion and staged the ignominy of His triumph. The irony of the events is unparalleled: the unconscious adoration of Pilate in crowning Christ's head with thorns and in pinning the royal inscription on the Cross; the raucous crying of the Jews, "We will have no king but Caesar . . . His blood be upon us and upon our children." How terribly history was to fulfill that optative when Jerusalem was sacked and the Temple destroyed! How beautifully history would fufill it yet again when that same blood descended on Christ's kinsmen to redeem them!

Here was a drama more perfect than if it had been humanly planned. Yet the actors were real men, unconscious of their roles. What better proof could there be than this of Christ's supernatural destiny as the Messias of the Jews and the Redeemer of mankind?

Probable indeed it was that Christ was the Divine Being Whom He claimed to be. But probability was not enough. Christ asked us to consent to give up everything and follow Him, and this one could not rationally do on the basis of mere probability. It was necessary to put away every doubt and to commit oneself without reservation. Christ constantly insisted on this act of unqualified faith as an essential step. Even the love of which He spoke was a love founded on faith. Merely sentimental affection was insufficient. That which would be so amply rewarded was not the act of giving a cup of water to the least of men: it was doing so for Christ's sake.

Before I could make this final act of faith, a full year and a half were to elapse after I had accepted the divinity of Christ as probable. Saint Matthew had not taken five minutes to make a total surrender! Trained as I was in the habits of skepticism, the act of faith was for me a terrible stumbling block. In a sense it seemed to be the surrender of that which I valued more than anything else: intellectual honesty. To make a subjective certainty out of an objective probability was a sacrifice of reason itself. Yet, paradoxically, it was a reasonable sacrifice: for how else could one consent to follow Christ with that singleness of devotion which He, as God, could rightfully exact?

That I did eventually make this act of faith is attributable solely to the grace of God. I could never have done so by my own power. The grace which I received was a tremendous and unmerited privilege, but I sincerely believe that it is one which God, in His faithfulness, will deny to none who earnestly seeks Him in prayer. I found Him to be exactly as Our Lord had described Him—a Father Who would not give a stone in place of bread, or anything but the Holy Ghost to those who asked for It. "Knock, and it shall be opened unto you."

The same thirst for a fuller knowledge of God's nature and of His will for men which induced me to search the Scriptures impelled me also to look to the churches for guidance. As I became more familiar with the personality and doctrine of Our Divine Lord, I felt the need for some living institution which would bring Christ closer as a Person and apply His

lofty principles to the circumstances of this remote age. I began attending religious services
regularly, often twice on Sunday, in the hope of
finding some preacher who, aware of the radical content of Christ's message, would present
it in vivid and concrete terms. My ideas about
life had changed radically, and I wanted to be
told how I should reform my actions in order
to make them consistent with my new beliefs.

I went to Protestant churches of nearly
every denomination — Presbyterian, Episco-
palian, Methodist, Baptist, Unitarian, and non-
sectarian. In none of these did I find what I
was looking for. Whatever the individual differences between these sects might be, they were
alike, in the manifestations which I saw of them,
in failing to insist on the inerrancy of the doctrine which they had inherited from Christ.
The ministers were content to be accorded a
merely human and provisional authority. They
required no explicit and definite profession of
faith. The Apostles' Creed was chanted emptily,
as if its content were of no importance. The
injunctions of Christ were handled as lightly as
quotations from Shakespeare and Carlyle. Lay
poets and essayists were repeatedly invoked as
lending authority to divine revelation. Every

member of the congregation was considered entitled to interpret as strictly or as loosely as he pleased the word of God.

Christ Himself was frequently discussed on a merely human level. He was congratulated for His psychological insight, for His artful leadership, and even for His sense of humor. His Messianic role, on the other hand, was deliberately ignored, and the dogmatic aspects of His teaching were casually passed over. More often than not, His doctrine about hell was soft-pedalled as though it might perhaps be a little out of date. Reference to the miraculous and to the order of grace was generally avoided. The sermons given in these churches were for the most part little more than homely disquisitions on self-improvement, punctuated with literary aphorisms and allusions to current events.

Rarely did these pulpit-lecturers invite one to drink from the chalice of Christ's Passion. Theirs was not the intense personal faith for which the martyrs had shed their blood. Rather than pointing to the way of suffering and sacrifice, they dwelt almost exclusively on the psychological benefits and the interior consolation to be derived from religion. They failed to emphasize that radical inversion of human values which had been wrought by the Cross on which Christ died. Instead, they appealed primarily to human wisdom and to humanitarian sentiment. All this they could have done quite as effectively if the bloody holocaust of Calvary had never been accomplished.

Disillusioned with the Protestant churches, I determined to find out what Catholicism had to offer. One day I went to Mass. If there be anyone who contends that in order to be converted to the Catholic faith one must be first attracted by the beauty of the liturgy, he will have me to explain away. Filled as I was with a Puritan antipathy toward splendor in religious ritual, I found myself actually repulsed by the elaborate symbolism in which the Holy Sacrifice is clothed. Having been nourished for years upon the illusion of a Divine Master enamored of stoic simplicity, I felt that the display of embroidered vestments and gilded chalices was fundamentally incompatible with the spirit of true worship. The scent of incense, to my mind, represented anything rather than devout prayer. The painted statuary I viewed, not with the eye of one seeking communion with the saints, but with the sternly critical regard of one visiting a museum of art. More than I realized, I was on the watch for the bogey of "Romanist idolatry."

While the quality of attention which prevails in Catholic churches during Mass is in truth a remarkable, and practically unique, phenomenon, it was one which eluded me entirely. In their thoughts, nearly all present were deeply aware of the invisible drama unfolding itself on the altar; but there was little external unity to be discerned. The priest, so far from telling the congregation when to sit or stand or kneel, carried out his tasks almost as though he were alone. The congregation, for their part, were not watching with scrupulous exactitude the movements of the celebrant. Some, on the contrary, were reciting prayers on mysterious strings of beads, which Catholics call rosaries. Others were thumbing through pages of prayerbooks and Missals, which, for all I knew, might have been totally unrelated to the Mass. Not even a hymn was sung to bring unity into this apparently dull and disconnected service. The sermon—the only thing I understood—was dry in content and dryly delivered. It was however, based firmly on the premise that Christ was God and His teaching the revealed word of God.

The most interesting feature of this experiment is that, while the Protestant churches left me with a sense of mere inadequacy, the Catholic Church I found in many respects positively repellent. I stubbornly resisted the emotion which swept through the edifice at the moment of the Transubstantiation; I refused to be taken in by the candles, the vestments, and the incense; I positively recoiled from images of the Sacred Heart immersed in flames, and felt a stern contempt for Catholic religious art in general. I preferred the cold chastity of Protestant worship.

This revulsion on my part I attribute not merely to the strangeness of the rite and to the Puritan bias with which I was affected, but also to a personal unwillingness to succumb to any religious emotion before I had answered intellectually the religious problem. I was determined not to let sentiment draw reason in its wake. Whether in choosing reason I chose the better guide I am not certain. Man's natural religious inclinations often bring him more readily to the truth than his intelligence, which is easily ensnared. There are many approaches by which God can lead souls to the Catholic faith. Mine was only one, and perhaps not the best.

Some time passed before I again crossed the

threshold of a Catholic church, and a great deal longer before I acquired an appreciation of the exceptional beauty of Catholic ecclesiastical ceremonies. In my senior year at college I began attending High Mass regularly on Sundays, and gradually mastered the complexities of the Roman Missal. Better still, I came to understand the action of the Mass, apart from which its trappings are meaningless and even, to some, distasteful. That year I assisted with great devotion at nearly all the special Lenten services, and was deeply moved by the chanting of Tenebrae. The most thrilling experience of the year was perhaps Holy Saturday, when I rose at five-thirty in the morning to witness in full the blessing of the New Fire, of the Paschal Candle, and of the Baptismal Font, together with the recitation of the Prophecies, the celebration of Holy Mass, and the singing of Vespers. These observances, however, were scarcely instrumental in causing my conversion, for I was already at that time a Catholic in opinion. Only the decisive act of faith was wanting.

Not until I had actually made my profession of faith did I yield to the attraction of Catholic devotional art, which I now regard as a most singular aid to prayer and contemplation. Nothing serves better than visual representation to make us aware of the presence of God and of our communion with the saints, who ever lovingly intercede for us. Once faith has gone before, there can be no excess of religious emotion, provided that it be of the right quality. One can not help regretting, in this connection, that sugary sentimentality has gained so large a place in Catholic religious art, perhaps as a reaction against the systematic coldness of Jansen and the Protestant Reformers. I hope, however, that a counter-reaction will not result in a form of art which ceases to emphasize the human tenderness of Our Lord and of the saints. In religious art, I have learned, devotional values properly take precedence over purely esthetic considerations.

Catholic religious forms and ceremonies, then, were of little importance in effecting my conversion. Far different, however, was the effect of my explorations in the field of theology. I read extensively in this branch of literature and discovered that theological principles were the sole secure foundation on which to base moral decisions, doctrinal tenets, and religious sentiment. Catholic theology is an immensely impressive structure, as few who are familiar with it can candidly deny. The men who developed its vast and carefully chiselled framework in the Middle Ages were professional philosophers in a sense in which John Dewey, Bertrand Russell, and even Alfred Whitehead—to name but three of the prophets of our day—are not. They did not leap suddenly from the pond of psychology or of mathematics into the vast sea of metaphysics. Their minds had been sharpened by years of the most rigorous discipline before their apprenticeship was deemed complete. Each of them, moreover, took up where his master had left off, so that scholastic theology was the composite product of many of the best trained philosophic minds which mankind has ever known. They saw far because they were not too proud to sit on the shoulders of giants.

Reading even the history of scholastic thought, as presented by such able modern exponents as Maurice de Wulf, Etienne Gilson, and Paul Vignaud, was a veritable religious experience, so splendid a light did it cast on the moral law and on the nature of God and the universe. Gradually, and after centuries of the most penetrating analysis, the infinite justice of God was

shown to be compatible with His unbounded
charity, and the sufficiency of faith was har-
monized with the necessity for good works. Human freedom was skillfully reconciled with the
fulness of the divine foreknowledge, and the
goodness and omnipotence of God with the im-
perfection of the created world. Believing in
order that they might understand, the medieval
doctors discovered that understanding made believing easy. Their wisdom provided the nour-
ishment on which my faith grew strong.

From modern presentations I went back to
primary sources. My mind rejoiced in the bold
eloquence of Saint Augustine and in the lucidity
of Saint Thomas Aquinas, in the sublimity of
Saint Bonaventure and in the shrewd penetra-
tion of Duns Scotus. Concurrently, I read some
of the Catholic philosophers of our own day,
including Father d'Arcy, Father Martindale,
and E. I. Watkin. In them also I noted that
seasoned comprehension and serenity of outlook
which characterized the great tradition of
Catholic thought. I perused nearly all the published writings of Jacques Maritain, and was
startled by his brilliant insight, from the van-
tage-point of his religious faith, into social,
esthetic, and metaphysical questions.

I listened to the public addresses of Monsignor Sheen, and in them I found expressed that boldly Christian view of man and the modern world for which I had sought in vain in the Protestant churches. My non-Catholic friends whom I introduced to the oratory of Monsignor Sheen were horrified that I should be seduced by such an outright demagogue. They protested that he did not give sufficient credit to the opposition, that he oversimplified philosophic problems, that he proved too much from too little. But I was not looking for airtight logical proofs; I was looking for a priest and a prophet. I was looking, if you like, for a practical, living proof that intelligent men in our day could regard the supernatural, the miraculous as a fact of experience without having to apologize to anyone for this conviction. I wanted evidence that faith and prayer could penetrate beneath the confused surface of economics and history to the realm where the powers of light and darkness clash in unceasing strife. Father Sheen demonstrated to me that the Catholic Church could still sustain and nourish the unfeigned charity and the burning conviction of the first Apostles, qualities which appeared to be all but extinct in the contemporary world. He taught me little about philosophy which I had not already suspected; but he taught me a great deal about the ways of God to man and gave me confidence in the religious conclusions which I had fumblingly reached through my own explorations.

Jacques Maritain and Fulton Sheen, more than any other two writers, provided me with a new social philosophy, suited to the metaphysics of Aristotle and of the Christian tradition, and capable of supplanting in my mind the political liberalism which corresponded with the metaphysics which I had come to reject. They made known to me the Encyclical letters of Leo XIII and Pius XI, in which the content of Catholic social teaching was so admirably summarized.

My previous opinion that the best government is that which governs least was, I noted, based on the philosophical postulates of liberalism. Liberalism, if it implies anything at all, implies the cult of liberty—the liberty of the individual person from various restraining influences.[1] The

---

[1] Here, and throughout the next few pages, I attempt to depict the pure type of liberalism, as it appeared to me during my collegiate days. I am well aware that, however broadly liberalism be defined, there will be some so-called "liberals" whose doctrines do not fall within the scope of the definition.

liberals considered that all virtue and progress were conditioned primarily upon freedom. To advance, they maintained, it sufficed that one should be free to act without reference to the directions of others. The heritage of the past was glibly dismissed as a dead hand, and the authority of the living denounced as an onerous yoke. Liberty, it was recognized, is conducive to change; and change, being deified, was identified with progress. The Nineteenth Century idea of progress was, in the field of historical criticism, the logical counterpart of the liberal conception of man and society.

In their doctrine of the person, the liberals borrowed extensively from the philosophical premises of Kant and Hegel, who had themselves leaned heavily on the political prophet of liberalism, Rousseau. The individual was represented as a morally and juridically sovereign unit, as an inviolable citizen of the anarchic "Kingdom of Ends." The more extreme idealists went so far as to place within each human spirit the ultimate source of all right, reality, and truth.

Each person being accounted an end in himself, it followed that society was an artificial assemblage of self-contained individuals, unconnected by any functional interrelationship. Both in fact and in theory, communal life became increasingly acephalous and atomistic. The subordination of man to man was decried as an intrinsic evil, and the natural diversities which cause men to be dependent upon one another were deliberately ignored. It was considered essentially degrading to be placed in a position of service to another; God was said to favor those who helped *themselves*. Any virtues which did not find their final cause within the individual fell into scorn and disrepute: humility, meekness, obedience, and fidelity were said to be the marks of feeble and dependent natures. Conversely, virtues such as self-reliance and initiative were inordinately exalted. The concept of human equality was indiscriminately applied to all matters. The political and social status of women was not differentiated from that of men.

The family, like other social relationships, was reduced to a mere legalistic partnership. The differences of function between its several members were blurred, and the authority of the father as the natural head of the household undermined. Marriage was represented as a bilateral contract terminable at the will of either party.

The political tenets of liberalism, like its social philosophy, reflected a gross overemphasis on the autonomy of the human person. Each individual being considered a distinct sovereignty, the very existence of the State could hardly be justified. Some theorists maintained that all government was a mere imposition, and the best government that which governed least. Others attempted to salvage the rights of the State by depicting it as an expression of the united will of its constituent members. According to Hegel, the policies of the State mystically embodied the "higher" will of the citizens, and consequently were not amenable to criticism. Rousseau, Mill, and the preponderant body of liberal philosophers, despite certain inconsistencies in their pronouncements, ordinarily vindicated the authority of the State by ascribing its origin to a supposed contract in which all the members had implicitly concurred. Yet sovereignty, it was affirmed, still abided in the individual to such a degree that each citizen, no matter how ignorant he might be (short of actual insanity), possessed an intrinsic right to be heard, directly or through his elected representatives, on every question of law or policy. He could not, according to the majority of liberal thinkers, be bound by any measure in the adoption of which he had not had a voice. Self-determination, almost to the exclusion of other factors, was made the guiding principle for settling, not only the internal affairs of states, but also the extent of their respective domains.

In opposition to this autonomism, the Catholic Church proposed a social philosophy predicated on a different and profounder analysis of the human person. While recognizing and respecting freedom of choice, the Church denied that human freedom was tantamount to complete self-determination. Man, it was pointed out, is dependent on his neighbor for both his survival and his development. Born into the world in a condition of extreme helplessness, he never becomes sufficient unto himself, nor is it desirable that he should do so. The family, then, is a natural unit, sanctioned by the reciprocal interdependence of its members. Larger social units, likewise, are natural and organic; and civil government is a necessary institution willed by God and required by nature for the maintenance of order within the community. The State is a sovereign entity charged with assuring in the temporal order the tranquillity, prosperity, and equity necessary for the proper fulfillment by its members of their respective destinies as human persons. A government, to be legitimate, need not in every instance be established by the voluntary action of the governed; and laws, for their validity, depend not so much on the concurrence of the governed as on their inherent justice. In the State, as a body corporate, the various members have their distinct functions, contributing in various ways to the well-being of the whole. To some the function of determining policies is specially appropriated; to others, that of implementing them. Some perform offices of greater dignity, and receive greater honors, than their fellows; but all, as human persons, have certain inalienable rights. The inequalities and differences which obtain in every organized community are as healthy as they are inevitable. And where a perfectly flexible social system can not be achieved, the "vocation" of the individual will, it was observed, be in some measure determined by the circumstances of his birth. The good life is compatible with a relatively humble position in the social scale.

The liberals, confusing novelty with progress, desired that each individual person should ar-

rive at his convictions by means of original
thought, and were exceedingly reluctant to admit that any particular truth, being founded on
objective reality, was incumbent upon all. So
disproportionately did they emphasize the importance of the material factors of "race, time,
and circumstance" that it was seriously contended that what was true on this side of the
Alps might be false on the other. In their flight
from dogmatism, the liberals rejected all stable
principles, and sought to make absolutes out of
doubt, diversity, and change. Some adherents
of the liberal school merely professed skepticism
as to the capacity of the human mind to attain
objective truth; others contended that truth itself was relative to the individual mind. The
idealists went so far as to affirm that both truth
and reality were subjectively immanent within
the human spirit. Even those liberals who al-
lowed that there was such a thing as objective
error were unwilling to concede that it should
be suppresed. The individual, they proclaimed,
had an inviolable right to give unrestricted expression to his opinions, no matter how absurd
or dangerous they might be. The propagation
of falsehood they defended, either on the naive
assumption that men in general would see the

truth more clearly when the correlative error was placed in juxtaposition (Mill), or on the cynical assumption that, so far as society is concerned, truth can be attained only under the form of a "counterbalancing of contrary errors" (Acton). In contrast to this teaching, Catholicism proposed a theory which, while encouraging the expression of original thought in matters which are properly the subject of opinion, safeguarded the integrity of those truths which were objectively certain in the light of natural reason or of divine Revelation, and were salutary for all.

In its educational philosophy, liberalism insisted constantly on the free expansion of the individual soul, as a sovereign and autonomous unit, according to its own inclinations. The benefits of acquired knowledge were cast aside, and each student was urged to discover, through his own efforts, his personal brand of "truth." Discipline and indoctrination were deplored; self-expression extolled beyond measure. As a result, the individual was left without principles, without character, and without moral stamina. In the progressive schools was fulfilled the prophecy of Plato: "The master fears and flatters his scholars, and the scholars despise their masters and tutors." (*Republic*).

Catholicism, on the other hand, without neglecting the importance of individual initiative, emphasized the role of external guidance in the formation of mind and character. The value of an opinion, it was remarked, derived not from its originality so much as from its veracity. Conformity with objectively evident standards of thought and conduct, it was maintained, should rightly be expected of all.

Unwilling to admit the existence of objective canons of justice, the liberals reduced all law to a matter of expediency. The State in their philosophy was confined to functioning as a mediator between the conflicting interests of rival social blocs. Law was regarded as a regrettable, if necessary, restriction on the freedom of individuals to do as they pleased. The very fact that it tended to assure order was considered proof that it impeded progress. Law was divorced and segregated from morality, the sphere of the latter being made purely interior and subjective. The light of the individual conscience was urged as the sole criterion of ethical right and wrong, and the categorical imperative, existing within the mind, was commonly invoked as the unique guide of consciences. Catholicism, by contrast, offered a theory of law consonant with the notion that justice and morality are objective values; that their principles are knowable—and to a large degree known—in the light of Revelation and of natural reason. The dignity of law, as the embodiment and guarantor of justice, was emphasized. The State, according to Catholic theory, had a positive duty to see that each obtained his due.

The economics of liberalism rested on the optimistic assumption that if every individual is granted unlimited freedom to gratify his personal desire for wealth, a maximum of prosperity for all will be the result. In the name of free enterprise, private lust for gain was permitted to override the most elemental human rights, and labor was treated as a marketable commodity. Production became no longer an exercise of art, but a mere expression of greed. In contrast to this theory, Catholicism urged an economic philosophy based on the primacy of human and spiritual values. The State was accorded a responsibility for coordinating economic undertakings so as to assure the benefit of all concerned. The dignity of labor and the consequent entitlement of laborers to form mutually protective associations were boldly affirmed in opposition to the exponents of *laissez-faire* capitalism. Private property was recognized as a right normally appertaining to the human person, and the inequity of a system which tends to concentrate wealth in the hands of a very few was fearlessly exposed.

In all these aspects of social philosophy, I found that the Catholic Church offered a vigorous and coherent critique of liberalism. Liberalism I was bound to reject because I had repudiated the individualism, the relativism, and the subjectivism on which it was predicated. I could no longer temporize with a system which at every point tended to substitute doubt for faith, pleasure for hope, and egoism for charity. Communism and fascism I had found intellectually sterile and in practice pernicious. Catholicism, on the other hand, possessed an admirably clear and progressive social teaching consistent with a sound metaphysics and with a Christian view of the universe. To the Church I was bound to go not only for my metaphysics but even for my social philosophy.

Admiration for Catholic philosophy, however, was a very different thing from submission to the authority of the Church. Conceivably one might be able to accept the greater part of the Catholic teaching concerning man and society and yet remain an independent thinker, without any particular religious affiliation. But I personally, as I have indicated above, felt urgently impelled toward a closer communion with Christ—toward a more concrete participation in the fruits of the Redemption—than I could derive from reading and thought, or even from prayer. Christ as an idea was not enough. I desired to know Him as a tangible reality.

Our Lord had not been content to come to mankind under a purely spiritual aspect, fitting as it might have seemed for Him to do so. He had not presented His elect with a perfect book and taken His departure. He had come in the flesh to the children of men and had stayed to walk before their eyes. He had thought it worthwhile to suffer as a man—to feel hunger, thirst, fatigue and physical pain. By His presence and example He had strengthened and encouraged His disciples. With lips of flesh and blood He had dispelled their doubts and fears. He had condescended to become a visible object of human devotion. He had permitted His sacred feet to be cleansed by the Magdalen's repentant tears, His holy countenance to be wiped by the gentle Veronica's precious veil, and His lifeless limbs to be held by Mary His mother within her arms when the last agony was over. With human words He had forgiven sins and with a human touch He had restored health to the infirm.

From me, however, Christ was remote. He was a figure in history who had died, arisen, and disappeared. It was as though the Word had been incarnate for a handful of men only, in the distant past.

Yet He had said that He would not leave us orphans. He had promised to remain in our midst. "Behold," He had said, "I am with you all days, even to the consummation of the world." Between Him and me two thousand years had run their course. What could bridge that gulf? A Church, if there was one, in which Christ continued visibly His ministry on earth.

Christ had founded such a Church. The Gospel was explicit. Because of your faith, He had said to Saint Peter, I will build My Church on you, and it shall never fail. I commission you to feed My sheep in My absence. For a lifetime only? No, surely for all posterity. To the

Apostles He had said, I charge you with teaching all nations, baptizing them in the name of the Father, of the Son, and of the Holy Ghost. I will send the Holy Ghost to guide you, so that your teaching may be infallible. The sins which you forgive on earth will be forgiven in heaven. Continue to enact the sacrifice of My Body and Blood: he who eats My Body and drinks My Blood will be saved.

Christ, then, had not omitted to supply this fundamental need of human nature. When He left us, He appointed representatives to answer men's questions concerning faith and morals and to carry on His sanctifying work on earth, forgiving sins, administering the cleansing waters of Baptism, and distributing the Body which He had immolated for us on the Cross. With His deep understanding of mankind, He had inaugurated visible rites and had chosen to confer invisible graces by means of them. It was thoroughly characteristic of Our Lord to require us to do small physical acts evidencing a little faith and a little humility, and then to recompense them with enormous spiritual rewards. It was part of the logic of the Incarnation that He should give Himself to us in Holy Communion, not only by spiritual indwelling in the soul, but sensibly under the appearances of the bread and wine. With ineffable joy I read that He had actually done so: that the Word had been made flesh not only for Peter and James and John, but for all posterity. One could still adore God visibly in the Eucharist. One could still be united physically to His Sacred Person—both human and divine—more closely (in a sense) than was Our Lady when she had carried the Infant Jesus in her womb.

Now indeed did my soul, like that of the Psalmist, faint in the courts of the Lord. The very pace and movement of the heart were altered with desire for its absent Lord. Not the heart only, but the whole body through which the heart's pulse flowed, was penetrated with the sense of exile and of longing for Him of Whom it had been told. The ears were impatient to hear the sound of His voice saying through the lips of His appointed priest, "Arise and go in peace; thy sins are forgiven thee." The eyes cared to look upon naught else if they could not behold Him in the Holy Eucharist. The very sense of touch craved to feel the trickling waters of Baptism. The tongue was dry and the stomach empty with hunger to receive substantially the Bread of Life. Where, O

Lord, cried out the bodily organs in unison, can we, even we, be united with Thee? In My Church, came the gracious reply, you will find Me indeed. There you will be united with Me as flesh of My flesh and bone of My bone, for the Church is My Body and the temple of My Spirit. Speaking to My son Paul after he had caused Stephen to be martyred, I told him that it was none other than I Whom he persecuted. When he was bound in chains for My sake, he sensed that he had in effect become a member of My Body, for he testified, "I live, yet not I, but Christ liveth in me."

From my most rudimentary notions of the Church, as I have outlined them here, it will be noted that I originally conceived of it as a visible and organic institution. The Protestant theory which reduced the Church to the status of a merely invisible society, consisting of the community of the elect, had no place in my thought. Such a society would not have answered the fundamental needs of which I have spoken and for which, I knew, Christ had made provision. The Church in which I was interested had certain organic functions, namely, to safeguard the integrity of the faith, to spread the Gospel to all nations, to enunciate the moral law, and to administer the Sacraments. None of the Protestant denominations even claimed to exercise all of these functions. They had reduced the number of the Sacraments from seven to two, or none. They denied the efficacy of the Sacraments, describing them as mere "signs" of election. None of these various sects, moreover, made any serious pretence to teach with finality the content of Christian dogma or of the moral law. For some of them faith was a word without content; others denied that faith was necessary at all. For many of these reformers Christ had, it seemed, suffered in vain the excruciating torments of his death. No debt of original sin, apparently, was thereby cancelled; no healing graces were thereby conferred.

If there existed any power on earth which could authoritatively declare what the Christian should believe and how he should act, and which could validly administer the Sacraments which Christ had instituted, there was no doubt in my mind that it was none of the Protestant sects. There was but one serious contender for the position, and that was the Catholic Church presided over by the Bishop of Rome.

Before admitting the claims of the Catholic Church, I exercised what I now regard as an excess of caution. I examined its credentials with all the diligence of which I was capable. I gave particular attention to the "notes" of the Church—those qualities which an institution fulfilling the Gospel promises must inevitably have: unicity ("that they may be one"), sanctity ("by this shall all men know that you are my disciples"), catholicity ("teaching all nations"), and apostolicity, which meant in effect historical identity with the original Church. All these qualities appeared to be present in the Roman Catholic communion as in no other.

I then asked myself whether the Catholic Church had exhibited infallibility ("He will teach you all things"). In order to answer this question I immersed myself in the intricacies of ecclesiastical history and delved into the complexities of medieval theology. I studied the decrees of numerous Councils from that of Nicaea to that of the Vatican, comparing them with modern Catholic catechisms. If I could find one inconsistency of dogma, one article of faith which the Church had been compelled to suppress or to retract, or one binding doctrine which was absurd in the light of reason or of natural science, I was resolved to conclude that there existed on earth no visible institution endowed with the powers which Christ had ostensibly vested in the Apostles. I read the most scathing diatribes of Luther and of Calvin: I found them eloquent but intemperate. Luther was illogical and Calvin inhuman. I studied the controversies surrounding Galileo in the Seventeenth Century, and satisfied myself that the Church had in no respect committed herself to geocentrism. I studied the controversies surrounding Darwin in the Nineteenth Century, and was astonished to discover that, even in the time of Saint Thomas Aquinas, the Church had declared it possible that the human body had been fashioned not instantaneously but by a series of creative acts.

The more I examined, the more I was impressed with the consistency and sublimity of Catholic doctrine. Through dark ages and enlightened, through ages of fervor and ages of corruption, under saintly popes and ordinary popes, the treasure of the faith had been preserved intact. Neither the sordid political issues at stake nor the worldly cynicism of meddling statesmen had been able to detract from the majestic decrees of the Council of Trent. Not even the greed and depravity of wicked pontiffs (of whom, be it known, I found but few) had been capable of impairing the integrity of Catholic doctrine. In peril often, the deposit of the faith remained untarnished and entire. When Pope Sixtus V, that energetic and high-minded reformer, had announced that he would publish and declare infallible his personal revision of the Vulgate, containing several departures from the accepted text, Saint Robert Bellarmine had warned him, you will never live to see your new translation published. Ten years later, as the papal version of the Scriptures was being set up in the presses of Venice, Sixtus was taken ill and died. His successor laid the fresh parchments aside.

Surely it was a divine protection which had saved the Church through all these centuries from the human failings of princes and prelates alike. Like the boat in which Christ slept, the Church was tossed by tempests, but was always safe. When one asked for an explanation, there could be but one reply: "Wist ye not that I was with you?"

Finally, I asked myself whether the Church had the appearances of being indefectible ("the gates of hell shall not prevail against it"). For nearly two thousand years, I noted, the voice of Holy Church had rung above the clamor of the nations. No fear of worldly opposition had silenced her, nor any desire to win applause seduced her. With uncompromising logic she continued to set forth the full content of the charter of her liberties. The temporalities of the Church were taken away, her jurisdiction over spiritual matters abridged, and her claims of indirect political power repudiated by jealous secular rulers. In many lands she had been divested of her teaching authority and her ecclesiastical immunities were insolently violated. The great powers of Europe, finding her yoke too harsh, had many of them lapsed into heresy. Yet not one claim did she retract. With patience and confidence amid calamities the successors of Peter continued to admonish a deaf, unreasoning world.

Yet that voice still spoke and by many was heeded. Empires had decayed, kingdoms had been overthrown, philosophies outmoded, and heresies forgotten. The strident voices of dictators rang round the globe. The air was filled with the din of wars and rumors of wars. Yet whither turned the eyes of honest men, dismayed by the spectacle of famine, slaughter, and appalling ruin? To whom did their ears, pierced by the anguished cries of the innocent, strain yet to listen? To the pale occupant of Peter's chair in the beleaguered Vatican.

Thither I turned also, to hear his voice, not with the passing interest of the world, but with that faith which, proving all things, holds fast to that which is good.

Questioning could have been prolonged indefinitely. No saint or scholar is wise enough to answer every possible doubt, or even every honest difficulty. But I recognized that the essential had been amply demonstrated and that the moment for action had come. I made an appointment to see a priest.

At the prearranged hour the doorbell of my apartment rang. Having been waiting alone, I went promptly to the door. A figure in black entered, tall, of modest demeanor, and slightly stooped—a scholar in appearance, yet not, I judged, a man lost in bookish abstractions. His face was frank and surprisingly human. What manner of man, I asked myself, stood before me? A madman who had thrown away his life in the practice of some strange and unlikely creed? Or was he a mysterious person chosen by God himself to perform on earth the supernatural work of Jesus Christ? I began my interrogation.

Brushing aside the social amenities, I proceeded directly to the point. The Catholic faith, I informed him, was very inviting but it unfortunately had a number of unpleasing and problematical features which would have to be cleared up without hesitation or ambiguity. At one moment, for example, Christ had said thus and so; at another moment He had said such and such. How did he, as a priest, propose to reconcile the apparent discrepancy?

My priest, however, was a busy man. He did not have time to waste in answering every hypothetical question which I was able to raise. He was interested, rather, in whether *I* was a good investment. After an hour's discussion, apparently satisfied that I had a fair acquaintance with the principles of Catholicism, he asked me almost impatiently what I had decided to do. I turned aside the question (deeming it a trifle unfair), and our meeting was soon ended.

For several days thereafter I did not see him. At last, however, I recognized that I had all the knowledge necessary to reach a decision. I met with him again and announced that I had determined to become a Catholic. He then instructed me painstakingly in the content of the Catholic faith in a series of thrilling conferences

extending over a number of weeks. I was ready
then, he said, to be received into the Church.

There were, of course, last minute doubts and
hesitations. The very finality of the act appalled
me. I would have been quite willing to make a
profession of faith on a merely tentative basis.
According to my best information at the present
time, I would gladly have declared, it seems that
there exist no reasonable grounds for doubt. But
why, I objected, does God require me to commit
myself for all my future days? I am young, and
have much to learn. Already, in the span of a
few years, I have changed my opinions many
times, and things which once seemed obvious
now seem false. The Mohammedans and the
Buddhists believe and are in error. Does it not
follow that I too, though certain, may yet be
deceived? Certainty itself seemed insufficient.
Desperately I asked myself how I could be certain that I would always remain certain.

In a sense, as I have said above, God does
demand that we go beyond the evidence of
reason. He declares, in effect, you must trust
Me completely, that My word is the truth, and
that I will not deceive you. Your childish wav-
erings, He seemed to say, were based on the un-
certainty of your own judgment. Now you must

rely on Mine. The waters of faith look deep and dangerous before you enter them, but I give you My word that I will support and not betray you. You may stand all day if you please looking fearfully down at the water. I will not force you to move; but by standing where you are you will not get any nearer nor will the leap become any easier.

I came into the Church like one of those timid swimmers who closes his eyes as he jumps into the roaring sea. The waters of faith, I have since found, are marvelously buoyant. Indeed, when man is clothed with grace, the sea of faith is his natural element.

I felt, in addition, a natural reluctance to take any action which would estrange me from my family and friends. The call of Christ must be obeyed, but I would gladly have dispensed with the religious cleavage. After becoming a Catholic, it appeared, I could no longer be at ease with persons divided from me by so wide a chasm.

This difficulty, like the other, dissolved as soon as I had pronounced the baptismal vows. I immediately acquired new and exquisite friendships based on a common seeking for the things of God. Nor were the old ties broken off or weakened. Through the love of Christ, I found myself drawn closer to the entire human family. They, on the other hand, did not turn away from me because of my conversion. Among my family and friends I found very little hostility to the Catholic religion. Most of them were interested, with an interest born of human affection, to learn the motives which had prompted me to enter the Church. It is in part for them that I write these pages, hoping to account for my actions more fully here than I have been able to do previously.

My first sensation after receiving the conditional baptism which the Church confers on nearly all her Protestant converts was one of freedom. Very little in this respect had been sacrificed. I had renounced only that which I firmly recognized as error. A tremendous amount, on the other hand, had been gained. Here was liberty to believe and accept and love with all one's heart without any misgiving or restraint. Here was unlimited access to the wonderful gifts which Christ had lavished on His chosen Spouse, the Church. As a member incorporated in Christ's Mystical Body (for Our Lord and His Spouse are but one flesh), I could participate fully in the liturgical life of the

Church on earth. And not on earth only: I was also united with the Church Suffering in Purgatory and with the Church Triumphant, where the saints rejoice in heaven. I was intimately associated with the holy souls in Purgatory, whom I could benefit by my prayers, and with the saints in heaven, from whose superabundant merits I could freely draw. They, whose works and writings I had so much admired from afar, now became all mine. My saints, I could call upon them at will and receive their personal attention. It was as though they had lived and labored but for me.

Having become a Catholic, I was surprised to discover that my conversion had scarcely begun. I had previously imagined that I would instantly embark upon a heroic course of action. I had imagined that I would not share the weakness and timidity which made the Catholic men and women of my acquaintance act so much like their non-Catholic neighbors. In this I was wrong, totally wrong. One's human nature remains, and with it all the tendencies of pride and selfishness which faith condemns. I find myself, as a Catholic, incapable of living without compromise according to my beliefs. Indeed my faith, strong as it is, has penetrated only a small portion of my mind. Many of my opinions, imbibed from an unbelieving world, are inconsistent with my religious convictions. My natural sentiments are almost completely unbaptized. When I am insulted, anger and indignation rise within me as strongly as they did before. When delayed, I am impatient. When treated unjustly, I revile and do not bless. The most ordinary works of mercy, such as giving to the poor, visiting the sick, and counseling the doubtful, are irksome to me. If I do them at all, it is in a half-hearted and ungenerous spirit which renders them practically worthless. Any heathen with a spark of natural goodness can put me to shame in matters of tact and human warmth. When it comes to the most elemental acts of public devotion, I am so embarrassed to appear different from others that it is a painful effort even to bless myself at meals.

Does that mean that my faith is void and unprofitable? Far from it. Brethren outside the Church, do not be scandalized by the frailty and ineptitude of Catholics. Our human faults, the whole burden of fallen nature, remain with us as much as with you. Your conduct is often more praiseworthy than ours. The sufficiency of which we seem to boast so much lies not in ourselves, but in Christ. There is no sin so hideous that He refuses to pay the debt for it, provided that we go to Him with sorrow, humble love, and confidence.

The acquisition of virtuous tendencies is a slow and difficult process, in which may of us will never greatly succeed. By the power of our own will we can to some extent avoid the more conspicuous acts of sin. But the evil, thus repressed, continues to live underground, and, unless grace be present, will exhibit itself in other ways such as the stiff-necked complacency of the Pharisees. The world will never condemn secret pride as bitterly as it condemns the shameful sins. But Christ condemned it more severely because it is more incompatible with love.

True progress can be made through love alone. By forgetting ourselves and living entirely for the glory of Almighty God we can unite ourselves efficaciously with Jesus Christ, Who offered His Sacred Humanity to the Father without stint or hesitation. When one lives completely in the presence of God and for His sake, commendable actions become easier and more fruitful. The saints are able to conform their actions fully with their faith, exercising the necessary tact and delicacy, because they possess the crowning virtue of simplicity. Their whole body is filled with light because their eye is single. They have acquired the spirit of prayer.

In the Catholic life, outward manifestations are always secondary to interior virtues. Even the most dramatic feats of heroism avail nothing if the spirit be lacking. The merit of Saint Francis consisted not in exchanging his knightly attire for a beggar's rags, but in being able to live a life of poverty and want with unceasing joy and gratitude. He loved God so much that he was incapable of becoming discouraged or embittered, even for an instant, in adversity.

As the past recedes into obscurity, I watch it disappear without nostalgia. I recall it with difficulty and without delight. The man who looks toward Christ looks always forward, striving constantly to become more worthy of his divine Lover, hoping to draw a little closer to Him in this world and, after a little while, to be united with Him in everlastingness.

To advance in the life of grace is to become more childlike, more conscious of one's own littleness and ineffectiveness and of the bigness and strength of God. Gradually, and after many falls, we learn how to cast all our care on Him Who has a fatherly care for us, to trust Him completely because He is all-wise, all-loving, and all-powerful. As one loses oneself in Him one learns what it is to wrestle against principalities and powers. At the same time, however, one learns the meaning of that peace which was the parting gift of Christ to His children in the world.

Through a gradual growth in humble Christian hope and faith and love one rises on the ladder of perfection. The ascent is difficult because the spiritual life is a continual struggle. The field to be subdued is as broad as the eye can see, and as one rises the horizons widen. Yet the struggle is not without rich rewards, even at the bottom rungs of the ladder.